Managing Credit and Debt

Other titles in the *Money and Finance Guide*
series include:

Building a Budget and Savings Plan
College and Career Planning
Finding a Job and Paying Taxes
The Value of Stocks, Bonds, and Investments

Money and Finance Guide

Managing Credit and Debt

Stuart A. Kallen

ReferencePoint
Press

San Diego, CA

© 2021 ReferencePoint Press, Inc.
Printed in the United States

For more information, contact:
ReferencePoint Press, Inc.
PO Box 27779
San Diego, CA 92198
www.ReferencePointPress.com

LIBRARY OF CONGRESS CATALOGING-IN-PUBLICATION DATA

Names: Kallen, Stuart A., 1955- author.
Title: Managing credit and debt / by Stuart A. Kallen.
Description: San Diego, CA : ReferencePoint Press, 2021. | Series: Money and finance guide | Includes bibliographical references and index.
Identifiers: LCCN 2020034300 (print) | LCCN 2020034301 (ebook) | ISBN 9781678200466 (library binding) | ISBN 9781678200473 (ebook)
Subjects: LCSH: Consumer credit--Juvenile literature. | Finance, Personal--Juvenile literature. | Teenagers--Finance, Personal--Juvenile literature.
Classification: LCC HG3755 .K25 2021 (print) | LCC HG3755 (ebook) | DDC 332.7/43--dc23
LC record available at https://lccn.loc.gov/2020034300
LC ebook record available at https://lccn.loc.gov/2020034301

Contents

Take Control or Be Controlled

It is often said that money cannot buy happiness, but millions of Americans today equate happiness with spending money. A 2018 study published in the journal *Natural Human Behavior* sheds light on this phenomenon. According to the study, people who earned $95,000 a year said they were happier than those who earned less. But the average annual income in the United States was around $48,000 in 2019. People often fill in this gap by running up debt in their pursuit of happiness.

Americans use credit cards to pay for meals in restaurants, travel the globe, purchase new clothes and jewelry, and shop online for whatever items make them happy. They take out bank loans to buy cars, homes, and countless other consumer goods. But not all this debt buys happiness—many borrow simply to survive in the modern world. In 2020 nearly 40 million Americans earned less than $15 an hour. They depended on borrowed money to pay for education, groceries, gas, and other necessities. Consequently, Americans in 2020 owed more than $12.2 trillion to banks and other lenders. That amount was nearly three times the entire budget of the US government. Additionally, Americans carried more than $1 trillion in credit card debt, an average of $6,194 per person. The debt situation was better among young people.

The average credit card balance for Generation Z (ages eighteen to twenty-three) was $2,230. While this number looks good by comparison, it represents a 22 percent increase in Gen Z debt since 2015.

Borrowing money can buy temporary happiness or ensure immediate survival, but running up a lot of debt can lead to misery. A 2019 poll by the National Financial Educators Council found that 72 percent of college students said they were stressed out by personal finances. Many felt they lacked the education and resources to help them understand the complex world of credit and debt. But it is nearly impossible for most people to live in the modern world

"We're in a capitalist society, so it's to everybody's benefit to know as much as they can about being wise about their money."[1]

—Dameion Lovett, financial expert

When looking for a credit card or loan do your homework. Read the fine print, know the terms, charges, and interest rates before you sign.

without borrowing money. This leads financial expert Dameion Lovett to write, "Financial literacy is important because it's pretty much one of the things that will encompass just about every aspect of a person's life. . . . We're in a capitalist society, so it's to everybody's benefit to know as much as they can about being wise about their money."[1]

Learn the Basics

As a young adult, you face unique financial challenges when actualizing your dreams. But given the right tools and resources, you can learn to spend wisely and live on your own terms. Understanding the basics is key. Credit cards are not free money; they represent money lent to the holder by a bank. The money needs to be paid back with interest. But some credit card companies charge crippling interest rates while tacking on exorbitant fees for late payments. And while credit cards make paying for things seem easy, there are consequences to running up debt. Failure to repay credit cards and bank loans leads to a bad credit record that can affect a person's ability to get a job, rent an apartment, buy a car, or even get a cell phone. While it can be tricky to open a checking account, establish credit, and save for college, you can live well within your means if you set smart financial goals, resist overspending, and approach debt armed with financial literacy. The sooner you start the better your outcome will be.

Chapter One

Where Do I Start?

Nagely is a sixteen-year-old high school student in New York City: "Right now I'm spending my money on clothes and food. . . . I'm interested in shopping." Rishi, a high school junior in California, has different priorities: "I'm buying a lot of sneakers. . . . I'm one of those guys who spends money on athletic stuff." Gwyn, a Massachusetts high school sophomore, likes Birkenstock sandals: "I started seeing them all over social media. A close friend got a pair and, after that, everyone got them. Everywhere in my Instagram feed, I would see famous people and regular people wearing them."[2]

Nagely, Rishi, and Gwyn exemplify the spending habits of the country's largest demographic—Generation Z, people born in the late 1990s and early 2000s. Nagely earns about one hundred dollars a month tutoring a neighborhood kid. When the money she earns is gone she asks her parents for more so she can pursue her interest in shopping. Rishi sells his used athletic equipment online and gets money from his parents to cover most of his other expenses, including transportation and dining out. Gwyn does not have a job. She shops on her phone using store apps and pays for everything using her mother's credit card.

In the lives of most Americans, shopping plays a central role in the lives of Generation Z. As Virginia high school senior Talia explains, "We've all been socialized into the culture of buying things as a social activity or to release stress."[3] This socialization adds up to big bucks for marketers and corporations. According to *Forbes*, Gen Z kids spent around $144 billion in 2019 on a range of products. But not everyone is like Gwyn, who has access to her mom's credit card. So how do kids pay for expensive products like mountain bikes, video game consoles, computers, and cars? Some save up money from their allowances and part-time jobs until they can afford to buy what they want. Or they might be among the 20 percent of American teenagers who have a credit card in their name. While no one under age eighteen can legally acquire a credit card, parents can list children of any age as authorized users on their cards. This means that although the credit card lists the kid's name, the parents are legally responsible for charges made to the account.

There are reasons that credit cards are restricted to adults. It is easy to get into financial trouble when using one. While it might feel painless to use plastic to pay for something, you are borrowing money from a bank to make the purchase. The cardholder is legally obligated to pay that money back to the bank, which is known as the creditor. This arrangement allows people with credit cards to enjoy today what they must pay for next month—or at some point in time.

People use credit cards to buy gas, groceries, clothes, and services like dental work and car repair. They also use credit to get auto loans and to apply for personal loans to finance home repairs, weddings, furniture, and other big-ticket items.

Many loans are paid back over a certain time period. A typical new car loan might require monthly payments for five to seven years, while the average mortgage can extend for thirty years. Credit card debt does not have a set length for repayment, but a minimum payment is required each month. Banks make money on loans by charging a fee called interest—a percentage of the money owed that is added to the balance (total debt).

Several types of financial institutions make loans. Retail banks like Bank of America, Chase, and Wells Fargo have branches in towns and cities across the country. Retail banks also offer checking accounts. Consumers deposit money in these accounts to pay for goods and services by either issuing paper checks or using a debit card tied to the account. Banks often charge a monthly fee for checking accounts or require consumers to keep a minimum amount of money in the account.

Retail banks also offer savings accounts. When customers deposit money in their savings accounts, banks pay interest on the money. Interest rates are generally low, less than 2 percent in 2020.

Smaller banks called credit unions offer services that are identical to retail banks. Credit unions are nonprofit institutions and require membership. Because they are not driven to earn profits, credit unions are often cheaper to use than retail banks. This

Credit cards make shopping easy, no need for cash in your pocket. But spending more than you can afford can cause serious financial problems.

means that most credit unions offer completely free checking accounts. According to the financial service company Bankrate, only 38 percent of retail banks provided free checking accounts in 2018. Credit unions also tend to charge lower interest rates on car loans, mortgages, and credit cards. Establishing a membership in a credit union is how many kids buy their first car.

Credit unions and retail banks have websites and apps that allow consumers to use them online. Another type of financial institution, the online bank, uses a website and an app for all transactions. These banks do not have physical branches where customers can use ATMs or make deposits with bank tellers. Some online banks offer free checking accounts, while others exist only to make personal loans.

Debit Cards vs. Credit Cards

Credit cards and debit cards may look the same, but there are major differences between the two. A debit card is linked to a checking account and draws on funds deposited into that account. Most people age fourteen or older can open a joint checking account with a parent or guardian and get a debit card in their own name. When people pay with a debit card, the money is immediately deducted from their checking account. There is no interest charged on purchases, and users cannot rack up unpaid debts with a debit card. However, if a debit card is stolen, the money for any unauthorized purchases might be deducted from the victim's checking account. If the cardholder notifies the bank immediately, he or she is not liable for unauthorized purchases. However, if the cardholder waits even two days to report the loss, he or she might have to pay the first fifty dollars in unauthorized charges.

One way to avoid problems is to buy a prepaid credit card and add a certain amount of money to it. Prepaid cards are not tied to a checking account, and they can be purchased at a bank or store. Some come preloaded with a certain balance, while others require consumers to add funds to the card when they buy it. Either way, consumers can use the card until the balance is gone.

Family Financial Literacy

Millions of Americans do not have a good understanding of financial matters like banking, saving, credit, interest, and debt. This lack of knowledge is called financial illiteracy. This problem is often traced to the way families deal with money matters. Advertising executive John Schmoll was someone who grew up financially illiterate. When Schmoll was a kid in the 1980s, many people, including his parents, did not talk about their finances, money, or debt. Money matters were seen as deeply personal; discussing financial obligations was considered distasteful. But silence is not golden. Schmoll later discovered why financial discussions were taboo when he was growing up—his parents had money problems, and they tried to protect their children from them. Schmoll's parents did not want to reveal that the family lacked independence, relying on credit cards and personal loans for survival. And the lack of candor about the issue left Schmoll with little understanding of basic financial concepts. As soon as he could get a credit card at age eighteen, he ran up $25,000 in credit card debt. This left Schmoll with a huge financial burden he came to regret as he worked his way through college: "I used and viewed credit cards as a way to finance the kind of lifestyle I wanted or thought I deserved. . . . I had very little to show for it when all was said and done. . . . I wish I would've known that you sign over your freedom when you willingly incur consumer debt."

Quoted in Ben Luthi, "What I Wish I Had Known About Debt: 4 People Share Lessons They've Learned," NerdWallet, September 25, 2015. www.nerdwallet.com.

Learning financial concepts and how to handle money is called "financial literacy."

Some debit cards are designed for one-time use and are thrown away when the funds are depleted. Others can be used continually; users reload the cards (add funds) when needed. The downside of such cards is that they charge fees that can quickly add up. For example, the Walmart MoneyCard charges $3.00 to reload at a Walmart store and $4.95 to reload online. The card also comes with a $3.00 monthly fee. And like many debit cards, the MoneyCard charges customers a fee when they get cash from an ATM. While the MoneyCard only takes $2 for each with-

The most commonly used credit cards are Visa and MasterCard. While they all look the same, they have different credit terms and interest rates.

drawal, some preloaded cards charge $5 or more for ATM cash withdrawals.

Credit cards are less costly to use if the balance is paid off every month. They are also safer. When a credit card is lost or stolen, cardholders are usually not responsible for any unauthorized charges. Credit cards are also the best option for costly purchases such as electronics or appliances. Users are protected against disputes with the seller if the item arrives broken or is not what the buyer expected. Is such cases cardholders can request a reimbursement from the credit card company. Some credit cards also offer purchase protection, which insures purchases against theft, loss, and accidental damage. And many credit cards provide extended warranty protection, which covers a product even after the original manufacturer's warranty period expires.

Debt Stress

Financial experts say it is best to use debit cards when paying for basic expenses such as food or gas. When a person charges groceries, a meal in a restaurant, or a tank of gas on a credit card, these things will be consumed long before the monthly bill comes due. It is better to use cash or a debit card for daily expenses. And running up large debts can be stressful. Credit card companies are not patient or forgiving when cardholders cannot make their monthly payments. As credit card expert LaToya Irby writes, "While the credit card issuer won't knock on the door for a missed payment, they will charge fees. They will also call, send letters, and may eventually decide to sue [take the debtor to court] for an unpaid credit card balance, no matter the amount."4

Millions of Americans deal with calls, letters, and lawsuits from credit card companies. Every month around 17 percent of

> "[Credit card issuers will] call, send letters, and may eventually decide to sue [take the debtor to court] for an unpaid credit card balance, no matter the amount."4
>
> —LaToya Irby, credit card expert

Building Blocks for Financial Success

The Consumer Financial Protection Bureau (CFPB) is a government agency dedicated to enforcing financial laws and educating consumers. In 2016 the CFPB released a report, *Building Blocks to Help Youth Achieve Financial Capability*. It focused on three areas that young people need to develop to successfully navigate the financial world of credit and debt.

According to the CFPB, the first building block is related to mental processes referred to as executive functions. Children as young as age five can understand good financial habits such as self-control, planning for the future, and juggling multiple tasks. Executive functions can be applied to developing good math skills, saving money, setting financial goals, and creating budgets.

The second building block is called financial habits and norms. These are learned by kids ages six to twelve. Good financial habits include managing money on a daily basis, learning to quickly resolve financial problems, and understanding systems to pay bills on time. The CFPB calls the third building block financial knowledge and decision-making skills. These are developed during the teenage years. These abilities include successfully researching financial options, comparison shopping, and making long-range financial commitments. As the report makes clear: "The CFPB's new research confirms the importance of starting financial education early and continuing to build on that foundation throughout the K–12 school years, and of financial education for high schoolers. Therefore, families, community organizations, and schools are important platforms for advancing these various building blocks."

Consumer Financial Protection Bureau, *Building Blocks to Help Youth Achieve Financial Capability*, September 20, 2016. https://files.consumerfinance.gov.

US adults are unable to pay their bills, including minimum credit card payments. According to a 2019 study by the American Academy of Pediatrics, these financial problems can affect children. Parents who struggle with high credit card debt can create long-term social and emotional problems for their children.

Kids who see their families stressed out over financial problems tend to avoid learning about money matters like credit cards and debt. And it is very common for children to copy the financial mistakes of their parents. According to financial planner Robert Young:

> Kids' money habits are formed before they get to high school and their parents are often their most influential teachers. It's unsurprising, but still saddening, that parents with troubling money habits seem to be passing them on to their kids. These parents are hit with the double consequences of their own financial mistakes and the prospect that their kids may be set up to relive them.[5]

Learn the Basics

Even if your parents are not the type to share financial information with you, you can still become savvy about credit cards and debt. For example, you can study credit card offers on the internet or look at offers that are mailed to your parents. This can be a daunting task, as creditors tend to emphasize the positive aspects of their cards in large type while using small print and complex language to describe the actual terms and conditions. Financial planner Yusuf Abugideiri recommends approaching credit card advertisements with a yellow highlighter in hand: "Have all the material laid out in front of you, pull out your highlighter, and identify the key pieces of information that you need to be aware of—the interest rate, any fees, conditions, things of that nature."[6]

> "Kids' money habits are formed before they get to high school and their parents are often their most influential teachers."[5]
>
> —Robert Young, financial planner

Untangling the details in credit card offers might be difficult. But this process is the first step in understanding how credit and

17

debt work in the real world. Whether you love to shop or restrict your purchase to the basics, credit cards and loans are necessities for most people in the modern world. And the teenage years are a perfect time to learn about the wise use of credit. You can start by learning the basics. The more you know, the smoother the road to financial well-being becomes. As Irby points out: "It's an exciting responsibility, but one for which [you] should be well-prepared."[7]

Chapter Two

Building a Credit History

All students are familiar with grades and report cards. A good report card might provide a ticket to a dream college, while a bad report card means you needs to work harder. After you graduate you might be relieved that you no longer receive a report card. However, grades and reports will follow you into adulthood in the form of credit ratings.

The financial affairs of almost every American are judged and analyzed by three major credit rating companies—Equifax, Experian, and TransUnion. These companies digitally monitor everyone's financial transactions at all times. This information is used to compile credit reports and issue scores based on a person's credit history. Anyone who wants to get a credit card, auto loan, mortgage, or student loan needs to have a credit report with a credit score. Credit scores are used for other matters as well, as certified financial planner Shannah Compton Game explains:

> Your credit score is . . . used for any type of loan you apply for . . . your cell phone contract, utility bills, private student loans, renting an apartment, and even some jobs are looking at credit score as a factor

of your potential as an employee. . . . A low credit score won't necessarily get you denied an apartment lease. . . . [But] it might mean that you will have to put down more of a security deposit.[8]

A credit score is also known as a FICO score, originally named for the California data analytics company Fair Isaac Corporation. A FICO score is a three-digit number used by banks to determine whether a person is creditworthy, or deserving of

While you may not have a credit score just yet, learning how to build your credit and establish a good score is important.

a loan. FICO scores range from 300 to 850. A score that falls between 300 and 579 might be considered a failing grade, or F on a report card. A score between 580 and 669 is comparable to a D or C grade, depending on the number. Around 21 percent of Americans have what might be compared to a B grade, a FICO score between 670 and 739. Around 25 percent of consumers get an A with a FICO score above 740.

The FICO score is based in part on individuals' income, the amount of debt they carry, and whether they pay their bills on time. A score above 700 is helpful when a consumer wants to borrow money for a big purchase like a car or house. Another benefit of having a good FICO score is that creditors will give a credit card holder a higher credit limit. This is the maximum amount of money a cardholder can charge on his or her credit card. Someone with a low credit score might only be allowed to charge $250 on a credit card, while a person with a higher score might have a $2,500, or even $125,000 credit limit.

> "Your credit score is . . . used for any type of loan you apply for . . . your cell phone contract, utility bills, private student loans, renting an apartment, and even some jobs."[8]
>
> —Shannah Compton Game, certified financial planner

Opening Bank Accounts

If you hope to get a credit card, college loan, or other type of loan when you turn eighteen, you need to prove that you are worthy of credit. This is done by building a credit history through spending and saving. And you can do this long before you graduate high school by responsibly using a checking account and savings account.

Around 10 percent of teenagers do not bother with traditional banks. They use fintech, or financial technology apps like Step that cater to the financial needs of young consumers. These apps try to provide more personal services than those available from large banking institutions. As Step cofounder C.J. MacDonald explains:

Schools don't teach kids about money. We want to be their first bank accounts with spending cards, but we also want to teach financial literacy and responsibility. Banks don't tailor to this, and we want to be a solution teaching the next generation of adults to be more responsible with money in the cashless era. It was easy with cash to go to the mall but now everyone is using their phone [to buy things].[9]

Wherever you keep your money, financial experts say you should set smart financial goals. One method of achieving this is called the 50/30/20 method of budgeting: 50 percent of your income goes into the checking account to pay for essential expenses such food and transportation. Another 30 percent is added to the checking account for discretionary spending, which includes travel, restaurants, music, movies, and other entertainment. Twenty percent of the money in the budgeting plan goes directly into a savings account.

"It was easy with cash to go to the mall but now everyone is using their phone [to buy things]."[9]

—C.J. MacDonald, Step cofounder

Spending Your Money

Many banks have checking accounts geared to the needs of teenagers. Most only require a minimum deposit of $25. However, those that allow customers to keep low balances in their checking accounts might charge a small monthly fee—around $12. These fees are waived if the account holder keeps a minimum amount of money in the account, usually around $500.

Banks offer a variety of options for spending money held in checking accounts. Account holders can use personal checks

Earning a Winning Score

College student Alyssa Cerchiai says she earned a good credit score in high school by opening a savings and checking account. She kept more than $1,000 in the savings account, used a debit card, and did not spend more than she had. She was able to improve her score by becoming an authorized user on her father's credit card. This allowed her to benefit from her father's long credit history, which included a record of on-time payments. When Cerchiai turned eighteen, she got her own credit card. After she moved out of her parent's house to attend college, Cerchiai used a smart strategy to further improve her score; she became the roommate who put the utilities and other expenses in her name. "[Giving money to] a roommate who pays for utilities or giving cash to a friend who took care of the check at dinner is not going to help you," she says. "Instead, take on a few of those responsibilities yourself—insist that you can grab the bill for dinner, and/or put utilities and internet expenses on your card and have your friends pay you back." While taking on the household expenses was intimidating, Cerchiai made sure she treated her credit card like a debit card—never charging more than she could pay off at the end of the month. By wisely using her checking accounts, debit card, credit card, and financial apps, Cerchiai earned a credit score of 778, which lenders consider excellent.

Alyssa Cerchiai, "I'm Still in College and I Already Have a Credit Score of 778. Here Are 5 Strategies I'd Recommend to Anyone Looking to Build Credit," Business Insider, March 12, 2020. www.businessinsider.com.

that are available for a fee. These slips of paper are filled out when purchases are made. When you use a check, you fill in the name of the recipient and the amount of money that the person will receive. You date the check and sign it. Your signature is a guarantee that the money will be there for the recipient when the check is cashed. Checks might seem old school; they are most often used to make payments through the mail. However, some landlords require rent to be paid with checks. And some small businesses do not take plastic and might prefer checks for payment. Additionally, checks help you keep close track of your personal spending.

People with checking accounts can authorize their bank to send a check directly to pay their bills. But most people forgo personal checks in favor of debit cards that are linked to their checking accounts. As financial reporter Justin Pritchard explains, debit cards "make spending easy; you can just swipe to pay, and you've got an electronic record of every transaction to help you track your spending."[10]

When you open a checking account, you are responsible for managing the money that goes in and the payments that go out. While banks do the math for you and keep an accurate record of all your deposits and payments, you need to compare the bank statements with your personal records. And paying close attention to your expenditures is important. If you do not have enough funds in the account when you write a check, the check will "bounce." This is technically called an overdraft, and it means the check will not be paid due to insufficient funds. Bouncing checks is expensive—banks charge anywhere from twenty-five to fifty dollars for each check returned for insufficient funds, no matter how small the amount on the check. This adds up quickly, especially since most banks still inform people through the mail of these bounced checks. It can take three or four days for someone to realize that several checks have bounced. Businesses that receive such checks might also tack on an overdraft fee.

Some banks offer overdraft protection to prevent bounced checks. If you write a check for more than is in your account, the bank will use money from your savings to cover the overdraft. Some charge a fee for this service, but it is much less than typical overdraft fees. There are usually no overdraft fees associated with debit cards. If you try to spend more than the amount in your checking account, your card will be declined by the merchant and your sale will be canceled.

Bad Credit Scores Mean Trouble

People who bounce checks or do not pay their credit card bills can quickly ruin their credit rating. And they can find themselves in trouble when they want to borrow money. Kara Stevens, founder of the personal finance and lifestyle blog *The Frugal Feminista*, learned this the hard way. Stevens was able to obtain a credit card when she turned eighteen, but she says she did not understand how the card worked: "I would just buy things and assume they were automatically taken care of. I'd open up the bills and

Bad credit scores can lead to higher interest rates; too much credit card debt can lead to closed cards and no safety net in emergencies.

see that the balance would keep going up even when I stopped buying things because I was getting all of these late fees. . . . It never really dawned on me that I had to actually pay the money back, and that the bill was a financial consequence, a penalty, for not doing it."[11] Stevens talked to her mother, who explained what was happening.

Stevens vowed to repair her low credit score, which hovered around 600. She visited the library and read several books about

Fintech for Teens

There are about 50 million teenagers living in the United States. Those who wish to create a credit history and start building a credit score can use fintech apps like Step, GoHenry, and Greenlight that are geared to their banking needs. The apps emphasize mobility, cashless transactions, savings incentives, parental oversight, and learning opportunities.

Most fintech apps charge a small monthly subscription fee. Parents can add allowance money to accounts while setting spending limits and monitoring transactions. Fintech apps also let parents create a list of chores with a dollar amount attached to them. When you complete the task and take a picture of your work, the money is automatically deposited into your account. You can use the app to decide how much of your money goes into a savings account and how much you want to spend. The apps issue prepaid cards that works like a debit card, and GoHenry allows users to personalize their cards with their names, such as GoEmma or GoNoah.

Schoolteacher Michelle Ibbetson uses Greenlight to assign chores like sorting laundry and picking up after the dog to her children, Dallin, age ten, and Addell, age twelve: "Every Monday, they get a deposit if they did their chores the week before. . . . It's nice, because I'm not nagging them."

Quoted in Ann Carrns, "How Parents Teach Smart Spending with Apps, Not Cash," *New York Times*, November 15, 2018. www.nytimes.com.

personal finance that were written specifically for women. She learned about positive money behavior and the power of good credit scores. She got a job and put her knowledge to work. As Stevens recalls: "I knew that if I paid my credit in full and on time, my credit score would go up, and that's always been my learning from the books. . . . I knew I was doing the work of getting good credit."[12] It took seven years, but Stevens raised her credit score to an excellent 766 by engaging in good financial practices.

> "I knew that if I paid my credit in full and on time, my credit score would go up. . . . I knew I was doing the work of getting good credit."[12]
>
> —Kara Stevens, personal finance blogger

Find Your Score, Protect Your Credit

If you are over age thirteen and have a checking account, savings account, or authorized use of a credit card, you have a credit score. You can check your credit score the same way adults do, by visiting each of the three credit reporting agencies—Equifax, Experian, and TransUnion—and requesting a credit report. You can also visit www.AnnualCreditReport.com. This is the only website legally authorized to provide free credit reports from all three agencies. (You should ask for assistance from your parents or guardian.)

To get a credit report, you need to enter your name, birth date, Social Security number, and address. Sites require users to answer a series of security questions. Everyone who uses these sites should be aware of several safety issues: Don't be fooled by look-alike sites. Do not use autofill on your browser's address line; type in the site's full URL. Do not click on links posted on other sites or in emails or texts. You can only request a free credit report every twelve months.

It is important to keep track of your credit score because fraud is rampant. More than 1 million children have their identities stolen every year. Criminals can use your Social Security number, birth date, and other personal information to apply for credit cards and take out loans. Identity theft expert Steve Weisman explains the consequences: "The identity thief never pays back the money accessed through the child's credit and the child is burdened with a bad credit report. . . . Often, the identity theft is not discovered until years after it first happens, which makes it more difficult to remedy."[13]

There are warning signs that your identity has been stolen. You may start getting credit card offers in the mail or receiving phone calls from collection agencies. The best way to protect yourself is by requesting a freeze on your credit through the main credit reporting agencies. This makes it impossible for criminals to get a credit card in your name.

A Wealth of Choices

If discussions of identify fraud, credit scores, and checking accounts make your eyes glaze over, you are not alone. A 2018 study called the Millennial Disruption Index found that 71 percent

Using apps to pay bills and make purchases is convenient. But make sure you protect your account from fraud and monitor all charges to make sure someone else is not spending your money.

of millennials (those born between 1980 and 2000) would rather go to the dentist than to a traditional bank. A similar percentage said they would be more excited to learn about a new financial service from Google, Amazon, Apple, or PayPal than from their local bank. Fintech companies are taking advantage of these attitudes by offering far-reaching services that offer everything from debit cards to personal money coaches. While some continue to visit ATMs at their local brick-and-mortar branch banks, others are building credit and paying for products in the digital cloud. More choice brings more freedom. But whatever you choose, establishing credit is a necessary first step on the road to financial independence.

Chapter Three

What You Need to Know About Credit Cards

Every day millions of Americans use credit cards as a convenience. Those little pieces of plastic give them instant purchasing power while freeing them from the hassles of carrying cash. You might be one of those people. According to TransUnion, around 8 million teens ages thirteen to eighteen carry credit cards that they are authorized to use by their parents.

Financial experts list numerous reasons kids should be added to their parents' card accounts around age fifteen. It encourages them to establish solid financial habits while building a credit history. As Junior Achievement chief executive officer (CEO) Jack E. Kosakowski says, "I view a credit card as a tool. . . . If parents use it as a teaching opportunity, it's a great thing."[14] Teens who use authorized credit cards responsibly will have a good credit score when they turn eighteen. Los Angeles mother Jennifer Olivestone Sieger made each of her three daughters authorized credit card users when they turned thirteen. Sieger says her children used the cards responsibly 95 percent of the time, and all had excellent credit ratings when they entered college. "We told them this is not magic money that comes out of nowhere; you can't buy everything you want," Sieger says. "They were only allowed to use the card with our permission. They knew I looked over the bill each month and if they bought something that was not approved, they would have to pay for it."[15]

> "I view a credit card as a tool. . . . If parents use it as a teaching opportunity, it's a great thing."[14]
>
> —Jack E. Kosakowski, Junior Achievement CEO

Transactors and Revolvers

Whether you have a card in your own name, use your parent's plastic, or have no access to credit, there are things you should know about credit cards. The majority of credit cards are either Mastercard or Visa, which are multinational financial service

Being an authorized user on a parent's credit card can help teens establish a good credit score.

corporations. Banks and credit unions that issue credit cards to consumers work with Visa and Mastercard to process payments between merchants and the banks when consumers use their credit cards. Visa and Mastercard branded cards are used to purchase goods and services online and at brick-and-mortar businesses throughout the world. Other types of credit cards such as Discover and American Express work the same way.

As Sieger makes clear, a credit card is a legal contract between the bank and the cardholder. Signing up for a credit card requires you to agree to the terms and conditions laid out by the creditor. When you use a credit card, you are obligated to pay

Student Reward Cards

Most banks offer student credit cards with rewards meant to benefit kids going to college. Some have unique perks tailored to the specific needs of students. Cardholders are not necessarily required to have a long credit history, but applicants must be eighteen to apply for the cards.

In 2020 the Discover It Student Cash Back card offered 5 percent cash back on gas, groceries, restaurants, and Amazon. And Discover matched all cash back at the end of the cardholder's first year. These benefits could add up to hundreds of dollars. Additionally, the card provided a twenty-dollar Good Grade Reward to anyone maintaining a 3.0 or higher grade point average during the school year.

Banks do not offer rewards out of kindness or generosity. They want cardholders to spend money, carry a balance, and run up interest rates and fees. That is why it is important for cardholders who use rewards cards to pay off their balances in full every month. If they do not, the interest on the balance will wipe out whatever savings might be received from rewards. A 3 percent cash back reward is no match for a 17 percent interest rate charged on unpaid balances. And prospective cardholders should make sure rewards cards do not come with annual fees, which reduce the value of the rewards.

back every dollar you spend, along with interest and fees that might accrue to the account.

Those who make credit cards purchases and pay off their balances every month are referred to as transactors by card issuers. As financial advisor Chuck Bentley explains, "To pure transactors, the balances on their cards aren't really debts at all, since any purchases will be paid off before interest charges are applied."[16] Transactors make up a little more than 60 percent of the population. The credit card industry calls the rest of its credit card holders revolvers. These people do not pay off their credit card balances each month and pay interest on the money they owe. Owing money on a credit card—and paying off part of the debt every month—does not necessarily lower a person's credit score. But carrying credit card debt is expensive. In 2020 the average credit card interest rate was a little over 20 percent. However, interest rates vary depending on a cardholder's credit score. Someone with a good FICO score can get a credit card with a much lower interest rate, around 13 percent.

Credit Card Statements

Whatever a cardholder's payment status or FICO score, he or she will receive a credit card statement every month, either online or in the mail. The statement shows all charges made to the account during the previous month. Responsible cardholders read these statements very carefully to ensure all charges made to their accounts are legitimate.

A credit card statement lists what is called a grace period. This period is the time between the date the statement is issued and the date payment is due. The grace period is usually around ten days. During the grace period, no interest accrues to the monthly balance as long as the balance is paid in full by the due date. Financial blogger Craig Ford recommends that cardholders ignore the grace period and pay their bill the day they get the statement: "[The] grace period is not an act of kindness. . . . They make it sound like the credit card company wants to buddy up. I've found that if I don't pay the bill right away, I'm more likely to forget to pay the bill. As a result, I pay the balance when I get the bill."[17]

Grace periods do not apply to balances carried from previous months. Whether or not the cardholder uses the grace period, it is extremely important to make a payment by the due date. Credit card issuers are required by law to include a late payment warning on statements that spells out the penalty for sending in payments late. Those who miss a payment, even by one day, will incur late fees that might range from $28 to $39, and their credit score can be lowered.

Credit card statements are also required to carry a minimum payment warning. This tells customers how long it will take to pay off their balance if they only make the minimum payment each month. Credit card companies earn billions in interest payments every year. And minimum payments are structured to ensure that this money continues to pour in. The minimum payment is usually around 3 percent of the balance owed. This might sound like a good deal to an inexperienced cardholder: you owe $1,000, but the creditor only wants $33 for now. But that minimum payment is applied first to interest charges. This means the balance is only reduced by a few dollars. For example, if you have a credit card balance of $7,800 with an interest rate of 15 percent and you make a 3 percent minimum payment each month, it would take nearly four years to repay the debt entirely. And the amount you had to pay back would be $10,153, equal to $2,353 in interest.

Millions of cardholders make only the minimum payment on their credit cards. And many who owe money on their credit cards are delinquent—they miss their monthly payment. This leads to additional charges. Late fees are added to the balance, the minimum payment increases, and the creditor raises the

> "I've found that if I don't pay the bill right away, I'm more likely to forget to pay the bill. As a result, I pay the balance when I get the bill."[17]
>
> —Craig Ford, financial blogger

n payment

t due date

imit

le credit

l interest rates:

ses

advances

Know your credit card statements. Interest rates on cash withdrawals are usually quite higher than purchase rates.

$10,466.40

→ 19.99%

→ 21.99%

ATING YOUR BALANCE

-$0

debtor's interest rate. As a result, the outstanding balance, or amount that must be paid for the consumer to catch up, gets larger every month. It becomes increasingly difficult for the user to get out of the hole he or she is in. That is why credit expert Beverly Harzog warns, "It's imperative that [credit cards] are used responsibly, or else it's going to backfire."[18]

Learning from Credit Card Offers

One way to become savvy about credit cards and prevent future problems is to study the credit card offers that are mailed to your house or are available on the internet. The key information on a credit card offer is contained in a large table known as the Schumer Box (named after Senator Charles Schumer, who wrote legislation requiring creditors to present standardized information to consumers about credit cards). The Schumer Box includes the annual

> "It's imperative that [credit cards] are used responsibly, or else it's going to backfire."[18]
>
> —Beverly Harzog, credit expert

Bombarded with Credit Card Offers

In 2020 Samantha Garrett was on the receiving end of a marketing blitz. Garrett received sixty credit card offers in two months because she fit into a demographic (sector of the population) highly prized by credit card issuers. Garrett was a college graduate in her midtwenties with good career prospects and an excellent credit score. Garret received, among others, six offers from Capital One, five from Discover, sixteen from Bank of America, and sixteen from Delta SkyMiles. The cards offered all sorts of sign-up bonuses, including cash back, air miles, and points. A card from United Airlines came with 45,000 rewards points and $200 in travel credits. Delta offered 50,000 travel miles. Bank of America included a $200 cash bonus offer. Garrett says, "I was amazed at how many showed up in a few short months. I found it very inappropriate to target me, especially being a student without an income."

If Garrett looked into the business of direct mail credit cards, she would not be surprised by the avalanche of offers she received. Credit card companies send out about 3.6 billion pieces of mail annually, or 300 million a month. This equals around thirty offers for every adult in the United States. The effort was wasted on Garrett, who had two credit cards and did not plan to sign up for new ones. But she might consider signing up for another offer. Credit rating bureaus operate a website (www.optoutprescree.com) that allows consumers to remove their names from mailing lists compiled by credit card companies.

Quoted in Steve Rosen, "Kids & Money: Credit Card Offers Stack Up for New Grads," Tucson.com, April 4, 2020. https://tucson.com

percentage rate (APR), which is the amount of interest the creditor charges on unpaid balances. The box also describes terms of the grace period. The Schumer Box lists the annual fee—the once-a-year charge the company bills cardholders (many cards do not charge an annual fee). Other fees include late fees and over-the-limit fees, charged when a consumer charges more than the set credit limit. An internet search for "Schumer Box" brings up flash cards, work sheets, and detailed descriptions of each aspect of the disclosure.

Choosing the Best Starter Card

Understanding information in the Schumer Box will help you choose the best credit card for yourself when you turn eighteen. There are several types of credit cards that are designed for teens, referred to as starter cards. A secured credit card is aimed at people who have no credit history or a bad credit rating. To obtain this type of card, a user gives the credit card company a security deposit, usually around $200 or $300. This becomes the spending limit on the card—users cannot spend more than they have deposited. As finance journalist John S. Kiernan explains, this type of low credit limit can be an advantage if you are building credit: "This deposit makes it less risky for banks and credit unions to issue credit cards to inexperienced applicants. . . . If something goes wrong, the issuer can just keep the money."[19]

Credit rating agencies view secured cards exactly the same way they do normal credit cards. Financial information is reported in a similar manner, and if that data shows on-time payments, the user's credit rating will rise. Those who use a secured credit card for a year can graduate to a regular credit card.

Another type of credit card, called a store credit card, does not require a security deposit. These cards are issued by department stores and big box stores, including JCPenney, Walmart, and Target. They can only be used at the business where they are issued or on the retailer's website. Store credit cards are also issued by gasoline companies like Shell and Exxon. These can be used to pay for gasoline, repairs, and other things at their service stations. Gasoline company cards usually have a low spending limit, from $250 to $1,000, but offer incentives such as small discounts on gas purchases. These credit cards are useful for teenagers when they start driving. And like all store credit cards, they are easier to get than Mastercard or Visa; they only require a "fair" FICO score of 640. However, store and gas company credit cards tend to have very high interest rates. The average APR for a store card in 2020 was nearly 26 percent.

A third type of starter card designed for teens is referred to as a college student credit card or student reward card. These cards tend to offer lower fees and interest rates, as well as rewards. The most common reward on a student credit card is called cash back. When cardholders charge goods and services, they receive a percentage of that money back, paid in cash. Cardholders might receive a check in the mail once a year, or

Research the best card with the best terms for your budget. It's your money so spend it wisely.

the cash might be applied toward the credit card balance. Most cash back offers are 1 to 2 percent of what is spent. Some offer up to 5 percent for specific categories such as groceries, gas, or online shopping.

Student credit cards are offered by banks because they view students as profitable future customers. They hope their cash back offers or special APRs will inspire you to choose their card and become a lifetime user. While the complex offers can be dizzying, you can save money and build your credit score with starter cards. By picking the card that is best for you, you can watch your FICO number rise while saving a few bucks every time you go shopping.

Chapter Four

Loans for Cars and College

Some teenagers get introduced to the world of loans and debt for the first time when they decide to buy a car. Others dive into debt when they sign on for their first student loans to pay for college. In both cases teens without a history of borrowing will most likely need to enlist the help of a cosigner. This is a parent or guardian who signs the loan agreement with the primary borrower—in this case the teenager. The cosigner's signature commits the person to paying off the loan if the primary borrower fails to do so. Owning a car is expensive, and there are a number of issues to consider if you want to get an auto loan. And you might be shocked when you sit down and crunch the numbers. Drivers are required to carry car insurance. Teenagers have a higher rate of accidents and pay high premiums for car insurance, in some states more than double the rates paid by adults. On average, the cost of car insurance for a seventeen-year-old driver in the United States in 2020 was nearly $6,000, or $500 a month. Payments on an auto loan for a used car might be little more than half that much.

Since you probably can only afford a used car, you also need to consider maintenance costs, which can add up quickly. An older car might need new brakes, tires, or a battery, or it might be in need of other repairs. Even minor problems can cost hundreds of dollars to fix. Then you need to add in the costs of gas, oil, tax, and license plate tags. The costs of these things vary depending on where you live, how many miles you drive, and how old your car is. But the American Automobile Association says the average driver spent nearly 80 cents per mile on his or her car in 2020—in addition to the auto loan. If you drive 10,000 miles (16,093 km) a year, that adds up to $8,000, or $666 per month.

Buying your first car is exciting. But before you sign or your parents cosign a loan for you, make sure you consider all the expenses associated with owning a car.

Sign Up a Cosigner

If you think you can afford the costs—or if your parents are willing to help you cover insurance or other charges—you can ask them to cosign. Financial journalist Miranda Marquit describes her experience:

> After compiling research about the types of used cars I could afford, and how my earnings from my job were enough to cover an auto loan payment, I approached my parents. My dad was willing to cosign on a modest car loan through his credit union. My interest rate—and my monthly payment—were lower because I had [a] cosigner with good credit. I made all my payments on time, helping build my credit history so that the next time I bought a car, I was able to get a good interest rate without the need for a cosigner.[20]

Marquit suggests using an online loan calculator to figure out what you can afford. For example, a calculator can show that if you can afford to pay around $290 a month on a five-year auto loan at an interest rate of around 3 percent, you can buy a used car that costs $16,000. You might have money saved for a down payment, which is a cash payment made at the time of the purchase. However, there are other costs to consider, such as taxes and license fees, that are added to the cost of the car. Many times car dealers, eager to make a sale, will include these fees in the total cost of the car. Joe Pendergast, vice president of consumer lending for Navy Federal Credit Union, offers this advice to prospective teenage car buyers: "Know your finances and understand what you can expect. . . . Shop around for the best auto loan rates and terms, and let [car] dealers know you've done

"My dad was willing to cosign on a modest car loan. . . . My interest rate—and my monthly payment—were lower because I had [a] cosigner with good credit."[20]

—Miranda Marquit, financial journalist

An App for Loan Info

Femi Adebogun was a seventeen-year-old high school senior in 2017. He was also a CEO and cofounder of a start-up company called Mindmap, a personality assessment app that helps teachers make better connections with their students. By the time Adebogun was eighteen, he was on to his third start-up, ScholarMe. This cost-free platform allows students to apply for every available source of college financing. They only need to fill out one set of questions on the website. Adebogun explains his motivation: "People are so confused about how to pay for college, and there are 400 students assigned to every one guidance counselor at most schools. We tell them how to do it, step by step."

By 2020 ScholarMe had attracted over one hundred thousand users and was valued at more than $8 million. But Adebogun is driven by a higher purpose than the desire to make money: "We do not want to harvest student data. We're building trust with our users, and we're focused on creating long-term relationships. We've tested different ideas, like a ScholarMe debit card, and people are into it. We don't want to help them just pay for college but also find financial health while they're there."

Quoted in *Entrepreneur*, "Meet 16 Teen Founders Who Are Building Big Businesses—and Making Big Money," August 20, 2019. www.entrepreneur.com.

your homework, so that negotiations will go much better, saving you time and, importantly, money."[21]

There are a number of reasons parents might be reluctant to cosign a loan. The debt is noted on their credit report, and it might lower their FICO score. And some parents might not want to be on the hook for a monthly car payment—or a massive student loan—if their kid loses a job or is otherwise unable to pay off the loan. And some parents might not want to commit to backing a four- or five-year loan.

Getting a Student Loan

With auto loans there are few surprises once the purchase is completed. As long as the monthly payments are made on time, the loan has a fixed term, usually 48 or 60 months. And when it is paid back, then you own the car free and clear. However, student loans are far more complicated and often come with unpleasant surprises, exemplified by the experiences of Ian Redman.

When Redman was in high school, like many other students, he had a solid plan for the future; he would attend his dream school, study hard, and get a degree. He even picked the place he would

Sorting Out Family Finances

There is little doubt about the benefits offered to those who apply for the FAFSA. But there are reasons that millions skip the process. Applying for grants and loans subjects students to a unique set of difficulties. The FAFSA requires children to work with their parents to report their sensitive and private financial details to the federal government. Many kids are unaware of their parents' job history, salary, annual income, and wealth holdings, which all must be included in a FAFSA application. This motivates some parents to fill out FAFSA forms themselves, leaving their children out of the process. As anthropologist Caitlin Zaloom explains, this can create confusion for students who do not understand how their college dreams might affect their parents:

> Families . . . rarely have detailed discussions about how the cost of college will have an impact on the family finances—the drain on parents' retirement accounts, how much debt parents will have, what they will need to do to pay their required share. . . . Parents are silent about all these issues because they want young people to be free to pursue their interests and develop their talents without bearing the burden of their own compromised histories or mistakes.

Quoted in Andrew Kreighbaum, "How Families Navigate the Growing Cost of College," *Insider Higher Ed*, September 4, 2019. www.insidehighered.com.

work after graduation and laid out a plan to build his career path as an intern. According to Redman, "I was dead set on my path forward. However, at 18, I wasn't thinking about the whole picture, including one very large factor: cost."[22] The cost of college was the major flaw in Redman's plan. His dream school, George Washington University, was one of the priciest private schools in the country. And the school is located in Washington, DC, which has a very high cost of living. Redman did not realize his mistake until he was accepted by the university in 2011 and started crunching numbers. He discovered he could cover about half his expenses through scholarships, grants, and low-interest federal loans. He would have to come up with the other half—$25,000 a year—on his own.

> "At the age of 18, I was about to take on $25,000 in debt without understanding how credit and debt work—I was financially illiterate."[23]
>
> —Ian Redman, financial program manager

Redman did not know where to turn. Like countless others, he searched Google for ways to pay for college. A website hosted by one of the country's largest student loan providers was at the top of his search results. Redman clicked on the flashy website, filled out an application, and after a quick discussion with his parents, submitted the form. He was approved for a $25,000 student loan within fifteen minutes. Redman picks up the story: "I hadn't spoken to a human being to answer questions about my creditworthiness. I had only a minimal credit history and had maybe $1,000 to my name between graduation money and my cashier's job at the local [supermarket]. At the age of 18, I was about to take on $25,000 in debt without understanding how credit and debt work—I was financially illiterate."[23]

The loan allowed Redman to complete his first year in college, and he followed the same course of action for the next three years. He says he was too busy with course work, internships, and college social life to worry about his growing debt. In 2016 Redman ended his college career $100,000 in debt.

Six months after graduation, he received the first monthly bill of $978 from the student loan company. As Redman wrote in 2019, "It was like a bomb had dropped onto my lap. I had no idea it was going to be so high. Just the minimum payment alone nearly equaled my $1,051 rent payment. . . . [I realized] if I only make the minimum payments, the loan will be in repayment until I am 44 years old."[24]

Redman says he did not write about his student loans to discourage people but to help them. In 2020 he was the national programs manager for an organization called Credit Abuse Resistance Education (CARE). This nonprofit group has chapters across the country that teach financial literacy to students and young adults. CARE volunteers provide real-life stories about loans and debt. Students are encouraged to ask themselves tough questions about their future plans and consider the consequences of taking on massive debt. As Redman writes, "If I had received a CARE presentation, I would have known to ask myself whether I was comfortable with the implications of having to pay back this loan. I would have known to ask the lender what protections I have in the case of major injury or loss of work."[25]

FAFSA First

While Redman made some mistakes, he started out on the right path—finding out if he was eligible for federal aid. This is the first step every college-bound student should take, and it can be done through the Federal Student Aid website (www.studentaid.gov) run by the US Department of Education. Students need to fill out a form called the Free Application for Federal Student Aid (FAFSA), which determines an applicant's eligibility for a range of financial aid, including grants, work-study programs, federal student loans, and scholarships and grants offered by states, schools, and private organizations. Additionally, filling out the FAFSA automatically qualifies applicants for funds from their state, and possibly from their school as well. Some schools won't even consider you for any type of scholarship (including academic scholarships) until you've submitted a FAFSA. However, you do not need to be accepted to a specific college before you fill out a FAFSA, as long as you are at least a high school senior.

Pell Grants are awarded through the FAFSA process. These grants—up to $6,195 in 2020—do not have to be paid back. Another grant of up to $4,000 is available through the Federal Supplemental Educational Opportunity Grant, commonly referred to as the FSEOG. This money is granted to students with the greatest financial need.

The U.S. Department of Education also makes low-interest student loans through its Direct Loan Program. There are four different types of loan with various requirements for eligibility based on the student's family income, the institution they plan to attend, and the academic year. The maximum amounts, paid over four years, range from $31,000 to $57,000 for undergraduates. Annual interest rates on direct loans ranged from 5 to 6.6 percent in 2020. Students are required to begin making monthly payments on these loans six months after graduation.

While the government offers an array of programs, many students miss out. According to a study by NerdWallet, around $2.6 billion in free college money was not claimed by the high school class of 2018. NerdWallet found that more than 1.1 million students who applied to college did not bother to submit a FAFSA application. Of this group, more than half were eligible for Pell Grants. The average student could have claimed $4,000 toward attending college. NerdWallet's student loan expert Brianna McGurran says, "All college-bound students should fill out the FAFSA, no matter how much their family earns. Losing out on critical financial aid is one of the biggest mistakes students make. Submitting the FAFSA as soon as possible should be as essential as the college application itself."[26]

> "Submitting the [Free Application for Federal Student Aid] as soon as possible should be as essential as the college application itself."[26]
>
> —Brianna McGurran, student loan expert

Determining College Costs

As with most other aspects of college financial aid, there are plenty of websites meant to help students figure out their eligibility. And all colleges and universities are required by the federal government to feature a net price calculator on their websites. (Search: "[school name] net price calculator.") The calculator discloses a college's total cost, including tuition, books, and room and board. While the results might seem shocking at first, students should not be deterred from applying to the school. As financial aid counselor Megan McClean Coval writes, "You never know what type of aid an institution offers. . . . Sometimes students are surprised by what might be available to them."[27] To learn about available financial aid, students enter their par-

The cost of college can be daunting. Speak with a financial aid counselor at school to see what financial aid is available.

OFFICES OF
ADMISSIONS
RECORDS
FINANCIAL
AID

ents' income, value of their home, and other information into the calculator. Applicants can also consult the U.S. Department of Education calculator, FAFSA4caster, to help them discover their eligibility for various loans.

College provides a ticket into the adult world. But few are prepared to deal with the complexities of borrowing huge sums of money to pay for an education. As anthropologist Caitlin Zaloom writes:

Many students do not have a strong grasp on what their education will cost them, either in financial terms or in how it might restrict their lives. . . . Student loans are likely their first experience with significant debt and the demands of repayment are far off; loans that students take on as they matriculate will not be due for another four and a half years. For an 18-year-old, that is a quarter of their lifetime.[28]

Chapter Five

Fixing Money Mistakes

When Shanté Nicole Harris was twenty-two years old, she planned to launch a career as a financial counselor. But Harris was forced to quit college and put her dreams on hold when she developed Hodgkin's lymphoma, a type of cancer. Harris spent the next year in hospitals and doctor's offices, undergoing chemotherapy and radiation treatments. She was successful in her battle against cancer but had a new problem. Harris had run up unsustainable credit card debt while fighting for her life: "I was just putting any and everything I could on the [cards]. Groceries, gas, you know. Whatever I could pay on the card, I did."[29]

Although Harris recovered her health, her problems did not end. By the time she was thirty in 2010, she had gone through a divorce and was unemployed. During this time she charged everything on her credit card, from her phone bill to day care for her autistic son. After a year of working multiple part-time jobs, Harris owed more than $60,000 on her credit cards. Then her luck began to change in 2015. She went back to school, got remarried, and found a new job. With the stability of a two-income household, she was able to fix her financial problems.

Harris and her husband took advantage of the numerous credit card offers delivered to their mailbox. Many offered what is called a balance transfer. This allows a debtor to move the balance of one credit card onto another credit card. Balance transfers usually come with a 0 percent interest rate on that balance for six to eighteen months. According to Harris, "Whenever [my husband] got an offer, he was like, 'put it on my card.'

As soon as one of us got the offer in the mail for 0% APR balance transfers, I would transfer as much money as I could to those cards. As soon as that promo was over I transferred [my debt] to another card."[30]

Interest rates on a $50,000 debt can be more than $1,000 a month. Harris's balance transfer plan eliminated those interest charges and allowed her to put that sum toward paying down her debts. After five years Harris was debt free. She continues to use credit cards but pays off the balance every month and is able to put money aside in a savings account every month. Harris offers this advice to people who are struggling financially: "It always sucks when I'm in the midst of the storm, but honestly you always know that it's not going to rain every day."[31]

Mistakes to Avoid

According to a survey by CreditCards.com, around 13 percent of debtors follow Harris's method for debt reduction; they use balance transfers to reduce their interest rates. (Note: balance transfers, even when interest free, do incur a fee, usually around 3 percent of the transfer balance.) And Harris's success story offers hope to the nearly half of American adults who carried credit card debt in 2020. Like Harris, millions of Americans are in debt due to unforeseen medical expenses. Others are drowning in debt because they do not make enough money to pay for necessities like housing, food, transportation, medicine, and other essentials. And the problem is not likely to end anytime soon, according to CreditCards.com analyst Ted Rossman: "Adjusted for inflation, average hourly wages have barely budged in 50 years, but some major expenses such as housing and college have [greatly increased]."[32] When people do not have enough to cover their basic expenses, many use credit cards to fill in the gap for necessities such as fixing their car or buying a pair of shoes for a job interview.

"Adjusted for inflation, average hourly wages have barely budged in 50 years, but some major expenses such as housing and college have [greatly increased]."[32]

—Ted Rossman, CreditCards.com analyst

While a person's situation might be dire, there are things to avoid that will help him or her prevent even bigger problems in the future. While you might not have your own credit card yet, you will likely get one eventually. And avoiding a mistake now is better than trying to fix one later on. That is why financial experts warn that there is something you should never do with a credit card: get a cash advance. Most credit cards will provide users with cash at an ATM. Think of it as buying cash with a credit card. And like anything else bought with plastic, it has to be paid back. But with purchases of food, clothes, and other goods, there is a one-month grace period before interest is charged on the debt. With cash advances, interest rates kick in immediately, and the rate charged for cash is often higher than a card's standard APR. In 2020 the average cash advance rate was 25.3 percent, about 5 percent higher than the average credit card interest rate. In addition, creditors charge cash advance fees, which can be as much as 5 percent of the amount advanced. Bank fees and ATM fees can also be imposed by the institution that handles the transaction. And the numbers add up fast. Someone who puts a $1,000 cash advance on a credit card might pay a $50 cash advance fee (at 5 percent) plus a $10 bank transaction fee. The annual interest rate at 25 percent equals $250, or about $21 a month. Given the costs, a cash advance is a losing proposition unless the money is needed for a dire emergency.

There are alternatives to cash advances on a credit card. Many banks and online lenders offer personal loans at much lower interest rates. But these loans do not provide instant cash, and they require a good credit score for the best rates. Those who do not qualify for personal loans—or who cannot use a credit card for one reason or another—sometimes turn to payday loans. These small loans provide quick cash to people who have bad credit.

Many adults find themselves in the position of using credit cards for everyday expenses, like groceries, instead of putting some money aside for such emergencies.

But they come with high fees and outrageous interest rates—up to 400 percent annually if they are not repaid on time. Payday loans cause financial harm to countless people who are least able to afford it. Financial experts say that people facing monetary emergencies should turn to loved ones or even crowdfunding websites rather than borrow money at high rates of interest.

Negotiating with Creditors

Around 13 percent of those surveyed by CreditCards.com said they would either pay nothing on their credit cards or had no plan at all to deal with their unpayable debts. But ignoring creditors is

Balance Transfers

Banks often offer new customers a feature called a balance transfer, which allows them to move the balance of one credit card onto another credit card. Balance transfers usually come with a 0 percent interest rate and a transfer fee of 3 percent of the balance. Balance transfers work like this: If you had a $1,000 balance on a credit card at 20 percent interest, you would be paying $200 in interest annually. If you transferred the balance to a 0 percent card, the transfer fee would be $33, meaning you would save more than $167 over the course of a year. However, if you miss or are late with a payment, the new bank will add a higher-than-average interest rate on the remaining balance. This happened to finance blogger Mike Greig, who was forced to put an expensive plumbing repair on a credit card when he had a severe water leak in his kitchen. Greig transferred the debt to a different credit card that offered a 0 percent interest rate for six months. According to Greig, "I thought this was a great idea, though I didn't bother to read the fine print. I was one day late with my first payment and got stuck paying 21% interest on the full balance on a card I didn't even really want." Greig learned his lesson; always read the fine print before signing up for a new credit card. And most credit card providers allow consumers to set up free email or text alerts about transactions and payments due.

Quoted in Gabrielle Olya, "How to Come Back from 10 Credit Horror Stories," Yahoo Finance, November 7, 2019. https://finance.yahoo.com.

no solution to financial problems. Those who do not pay their bills incur late fees, higher interest rates, and damage to their credit. After several months of nonpayment, creditors will send the account to a collection agency that might use aggressive tactics to collect the debt. Collection agents will call—and even visit—a borrower's home and workplace. Collectors might try to get money from a debtor's family and friends. If a debt is still not repaid, the lender can take the borrower to court and demand a portion of the person's wages every month.

Credit card companies make more money keeping customers, rather than suing them or paying debt collectors to harass people. Creditors would much rather negotiate with customers and work out payment plans that are beneficial to both parties. Someone who is in financial trouble should contact his or her creditor immediately. By calling the phone number on the back of their credit card, debtors can speak to a customer service agent who deals with alternative payment arrangements. Financial counselor Roslyn Lash recommends that a debtor write out a few talking points that can be referred to when talking to the agent. "This one sheet, easy reference paper will help you organize your thoughts to stay on track," says Lash. "You're calling the creditors and they have a job to do, as quickly as possible. Putting it all on paper this way will help you not ramble or provide unnecessary information."[33]

Agreeing to a Settlement

Individuals might be anxious or upset when calling their credit card company. But they should remember that customer service agents regularly deal with people who are facing similar problems. In general, the agent will offer three types of settlements. Those who are employed but find themselves unable to pay their credit card bills can enter into a settlement called a workout agreement. With this settlement a creditor might lower the debtor's interest rate or even waive interest charges. The agent could also agree to lower the minimum payment and erase past late fees.

With a workout agreement the creditor might close the account as part of the deal, and this would further lower the individual's credit score. According to Lash, it is important for debtors to be completely honest about their expenses when setting up a workout agreement: "[Your] budget should be your bare-bones expenses. A creditor won't want to reduce your payment or make an adjustment if you are spending money on luxury items. Also, if you request a specific payment amount, it should be evident that you can make the payment without becoming delinquent."[34]

A second type of settlement is called a hardship agreement. This plan is meant to help those who are suffering from temporary problems due to accident, illness, divorce, natural disaster, or other hardship. Each creditor offers its own version of a hardship agreement, which can be often be found on their websites. Usually, hardship agreements are only available to those who have a solid credit history with the company. As with a workout agreement, creditors offer lower interest rates, suspended late fees, and reduced minimum payments to those who enter into a hardship plan. Debtors might be required to set up an automatic payment plan from their bank account so the creditor knows it will get paid.

Some who are trying to settle their credit card debts enter into what is called a lump-sum settlement. In this situation, the debtor offers to clear up a large debt with a smaller amount of money paid all at once. For example, if someone owes $3,000 in charges, interest, and fees on a credit card, they might ask the bank to accept a one-time payment of $2,000 to settle the account in full. Lump-sum payments are not an easy way out of debt for an obvious reason; most people who are unable to

Payday Loans

Payday loans are so named because they are seen as a way borrowers can cover emergency expenses until they receive their paychecks. Anyone over age eighteen can get a payday loan, as long as the person can prove he or she is employed. The borrower writes a personal check to the payday lender for the amount of the loan plus a fee—anywhere from $15 to $30 on every $100 borrowed. This fee equals 15 to 30 percent interest charged on a loan every two weeks. The lender does not cash the check until an agreed-upon date—usually the borrower's next payday.

There are more than twenty-three thousand payday lenders operating in the United States, more than twice the number of McDonald's restaurants. Payday loan stores are most often located in poor neighborhoods, where their signs advertise that they offer easy credit and cash in minutes. Payday loans are sometimes called predatory loans because lenders prey on vulnerable people with low incomes and bad credit scores. And this group includes members of Generation Z, as government reform advocate Abbey Meller writes: "Payday lenders have a green light to exploit borrowers and have set their sights on a new target: debt-burdened young people." The targeting works. According to the Pew Charitable Trusts, while only 6 percent of Americans used payday lenders from 2015 to 2020, the majority of those people were aged eighteen to twenty-four.

Abbey Meller, "Young People Are Payday Lenders' Newest Prey," Center for American Progress, December 23, 2019. www.americanprogress.org.

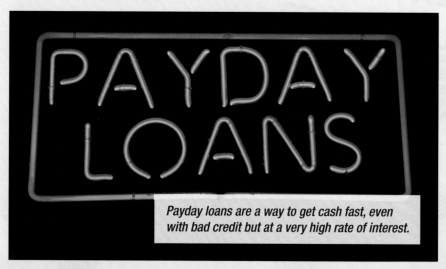

Payday loans are a way to get cash fast, even with bad credit but at a very high rate of interest.

pay off their cards do not have thousands of dollars available to settle their accounts.

While all financial experts recommend that debtors negotiate with credit card companies when they cannot pay their bills, many people are unaware of this option. Only around 7 percent of those surveyed by CreditCards.com said they planned to call their card issuers and ask for a break. But this is the

Negotiating and creating a payment plan with a credit card company can help settle accounts that are out of control.

best way to address money mistakes and take the first steps toward a better financial future. This is especially true for those who obtained their first credit cards when they turned eighteen and then misused them. Credit card companies deliberately target these people who might not consider the consequences of running up huge debts. "Credit card companies have been pursuing teenagers," says credit counselor Gary Herman. "Most teenagers don't fully understand the repercussions of using a credit card and the impact it can have on their future financial situations."[35]

"Most teenagers don't fully understand the repercussions of using a credit card and the impact it can have on their future financial situations."[35]

—Gary Herman, credit counselor

Chapter Six

Practice Makes Perfect

In 2018 financial researcher Ashley LeBaron wanted to understand how young adults had learned to manage money from their parents. LeBaron interviewed more than one hundred college students to discover what their parents taught them about money. Parents and grandparents of students were also interviewed to find out how they taught their kids about financial matters. The results were compiled in a paper called "Practice Makes Perfect." LeBaron describes her findings: "Let [kids] make mistakes so you can help them learn from them, and help them develop habits before they're on their own, when the consequences are a lot bigger and they're dealing with larger amounts of money."[36]

Most students LeBaron interviewed had some experience with money in their youth. The study showed that the kids learned several things from their parents, including how to work hard, how to manage money, and how to spend wisely. Parents who provided these lessons said they wanted their children to practice financial skills so they could learn from their mistakes and become independent young adults.

Some who took part in LeBaron's study did not receive practical advice about money when they were growing up and regretted missing out. LeBaron found that this group was not given the same degree of hands-on experience with money as their parents and grandparents had experienced. LeBaron believes that the parents of the inexperienced kids did not trust them with money, and this could be a problem: "I think it's hard for parents, sometimes, to let their kids make mistakes. It's tempting to just shield kids from everything related to money, but it's really important for parents to get money into kids' hands early on so they can practice . . . [and] learn important lessons about money."[37]

> "Let [kids] make mistakes so you can help them learn from them, and help them develop habits before they're on their own, when the consequences are a lot bigger."[36]
>
> —Ashley LeBaron, financial researcher

Training the Brain

One of the best ways you can practice handling money is to set up a budget. This allows you to regularly assess your financial health. Budgets help you evaluate your spending every month and make sure your debt is manageable. When you list your income and necessary expenses, the budget provides a snapshot of where your money goes. This might reveal areas where you can save money; for example, by cutting back on unused online subscriptions that renew automatically every month. For some, budgets reveal problems like an overreliance on credit cards to cover shortfalls.

When making a budget, you can separate your wants from your needs. Necessary expenses, or needs, would be things like books, clothes, and food. Wants are nonessential items that might include items like a bicycle or pricey restaurant meal. Or you might have your sights set on big-ticket items like a car or a cross-country trip. Whatever your wants, you can learn the value of money by setting goals and learning to save. And this can have long-term benefits, as personal finance reporter Liz

#1: Check your account on-line often.

Track your deposits and spending on-line daily. Use your banking app to track your debit card and check charges and your deposits. You may be surprised that your internal accounting does not match with the bank. The app will also help you keep track of what you are spending your money on.

#2: Understand how to budget.

Budgeting is the act of making sure you're anticipating your expenses and tracking them against your income. A good budget will cover your bills and expenses while also leaving money for fun and savings. Keep track of whether your budget is realistic or you are always falling short.

#3: Your credit score matters.

While you may not have a credit history as a teenager, building credit becomes increasingly more important as you get older. If you ever want to buy a home, finance a car, or borrow money to start a business, you'll need a good credit score and an active credit history. Paying your bills on time and using credit responsibly contribute to a good credit score.

#4: Know how credit card interest works.

Credit cards typically carry an interest rate of 15 percent or more. This is charged monthly on your credit card balance. Paying the minimum amount due means your next bill will include an interest rate charge. Paying your bill in full each month avoids the interest rate charge.

#5: Minimize debt.

You might have to borrow money at certain times to purchase a car or a house, maybe open your own business. Credit cards and personal loans can create bad habits and debt and can quickly lead to payments that you cannot handle. It is best to minimize borrowing and control spending.

#6: Invest early.

Investing early, even in small amounts can grow your money. Understanding the basics of investments and interest can help your money grow.

#7: Plan for emergencies with savings.

It is ideal to have 3–6 months of expenses saved in case of emergency. While that may not be possible right away a good goal is to save every month to build a savings account/emergency fund to help you in hard times.

Source: CouponChief.com LLC, 774 Mays Blvd #10-528, Incline Village, NV 89451. www.couponchief.com.

Knueven writes: "Start [saving] while you're young, though, and you might develop some good, lifelong habits."[38]

Saving money for a wanted item is not easy, even for those who cultivate good habits. There are so many advertisements by companies competing for your dollars that it can be hard to resist frivolous spending. Some people have the self-control necessary to resist the spending temptation. But even those who lack self-control can practice to become more responsible spenders. This can be done by repeating positive phrases that remind you of your savings goals. For example, you might say: I am going to go to Starbucks less often in order to save up for an item I want. If you say this rule of thumb over and over after setting a savings goal, you might stick to it—or you might choose not to. But psychological studies have shown that people feel good about themselves if they follow a rule, even if it is one they created. But the rule of thumb can work both ways.

Some people reinforce bad behavior by repeating negative statements. For example, you might be tempted to undermine your new vow by saying something like: I have so much work to do for school, I deserve a Starbucks Frappuccino today. Better to phrase it like this: I know that I won't be able to set my savings goal if I go to Starbucks now. Is it worth it? Or should I just make myself something at home and save the money?

Positive reinforcement is also helpful for people who are trying to pay down large debts. Professor of finance Hersh Shefrin explains why this process works: "Good habits do end-runs around the parts of our personality that give in to temptation. . . . If we identify ourselves as responsible, and take pride in living up to the virtues associated with that identity, then we activate reward centers in the brain associated with goal achievement."[39]

> "Start [saving] while you're young . . . and you might develop some good, lifelong habits."[38]
>
> —Liz Knueven, personal finance reporter

Apps for Financial Health

The banking app Wallit has features that make it fun to save for purchases while reinforcing the reward centers in the brain. The Wallit savings goal allows users to enter a product they want to buy, along with a link to the store where it is sold. Users set the purchase price and choose an end date when enough money will be saved to buy the product. The goal can be shared with parents through the app or via text, Facebook, WhatsApp, or email. Savings goals can be small, like dining out at a fancy restaurant, or they can be applied to major purchases such as a new computer. Whatever the goal, the user can set a very specific budget. When money is deposited into the account, a predetermined percentage is automatically added to the savings account.

The app FinX Hub can be used for saving money, but its main goal is to help users practice and perfect their financial maneuvers. FinX Hub offers a host of financial information through news feeds, videos, articles, quizzes, and even competitions that award prizes. The app was designed by Douglas Avery when he was about to enter college in Virginia in 2017. Avery wanted to learn more about financial matters but was not happy with what he found: "Nowadays you have [financial literacy] entrepreneurs who have courses they'll sell you. I went through every route out there with that, and I wasn't a fan of it."[40] Avery found that most courses that covered finance were not of good value: they were pricey and not very informative. Even worse, the courses were boring. Avery decided to build FinX Hub specifically to provide financial education to those aged seventeen to twenty-five: "We decided we wanted to change the industry, because it seemed like it was kind of stalling out on us."[41]

Users can personally interact with Avery and his team, socialize with other users, and learn about credit cards, borrowing, debt, saving, and other matters. And the app is free. Avery describes what drove him to create FinX Hub: "We want to bring financial literacy to the pockets of those that don't really have the guidance or the assets that we believe a young person should have."[42]

Financial Advice on TikTok

The TikTok video-sharing app was launched internationally in 2017. By 2020 TikTok had been downloaded 1.5 billion times, including 100 million downloads in the United States. The popular app is known for lip-synch videos, challenges, and silly dance videos. But the money-related hashtag #invest had nearly 30 million views in 2019, while #personalfinance attracted over 12 million. And some TikTokers are racking up views by offering financial advice about interest rates and credit cards.

Zack Zorn, a twenty-five-year-old entrepreneur from San Diego, has attracted over two hundred thousand views with his fifteen-second videos about using credit cards wisely to build up a credit score. Zorn was amazed by the feedback from viewers: "People were commenting they didn't realize they weren't supposed to pay just the minimum [required payment]. That's when the light really came on [that] we can educate people and help the people who are not getting the financial education I grew up getting." Zorn admits that his videos are only meant to offer broad overviews of a topic. But he believes that he is filling a demand for honest advice that is seriously lacking in the lives of many young viewers. Only half of American states require high schoolers to take financial literacy classes. And Zorn points out that students are often the targets of fraud: "I think there's a lot of scamming-type content online, and I want to be the opposite of that."

Quoted in Andrew Keshner, "The Newest Frontier for Financial Advice: TikTok," MarketWatch, December 10, 2019. www.marketwatch.com.

Pay Attention

Developing good habits is important, but life takes practice. You might not do so well with savings, credit, and debt the first time out. But learning from mistakes—and learning to correct them— is all part of the process. And those who slip up should remember that they are not alone. Even financial experts get tripped up sometimes. Melissa Lambarena is one such expert. She writes about credit cards for NerdWallet and covers personal finance in a column for the Associated Press. But Lambarena's credit score suffered when she pushed her credit limit to the max.

Experts say individuals should never use more than 30 percent of their credit limit. Those who go above this are given a lower credit score, which makes it harder for them to get the best interest rates. As Lambarena explains, "They offer you a credit limit, but you may get dinged when you use it all. In my experience, I've never received a notification, alert or information on my statement that tells me when [I might be in trouble]. Unless you go looking for this information or check your credit score, you probably won't find out how it impacts your credit and you might keep making that mistake."[43]

Credit Counseling

Most people are not authorities on credit cards and finance. And some struggle with insufficient income, overdue bills, and unmanageable student loan payments. Many borrow money for college and are lured into debt by the dozens of credit card applications they receive. Some are fooled into overspending by not understanding how credit cards work. These prescriptions for financial disaster have gotten so many into trouble that there is an entire industry focused on helping people deal with their money problems.

Credit counseling organizations advise people on their money, debts, and budgets. While some charge for this service, nonprofit credit counseling agencies offer free or low-cost advice to those who have made serious financial errors. Credit counselors are usually certified and trained to deal with credit cards, mortgages, and other types of loans.

First-time visitors to credit counselors receive an overview of their financial situation. They learn about debt consolidation, which entails taking out a single low-interest loan to pay off all credit cards and other high-interest debts. People who have more debts than they can possibly pay off might be counseled to declare bankruptcy. During this process, debtors go before a judge who eliminates their immediate debts and works out a repayment plan with creditors.

Getting control of your spending may include cutting up your credit card.

Some credit counselors focus on student loans. They emphasize contacting creditors to ask for lower interest rates or finding ways to refinance loans. People who have trouble paying their rent or the mortgage on their home can participate in housing counseling. These sessions provide debtors with options for managing their housing costs.

Sacrificing for Financial Freedom

Paying off large debts requires a person to develop a good plan and use positive reinforcement to stick to his or her goals. Twenty-eight-year-old New York City resident Mandy Velez exemplifies this strategy. Velez graduated from college in 2013 owing more than $102,000 on a student loan. She wanted to pay down her debt and get a second chance, which meant working tirelessly. When she finally paid off her debt, she held a mock funeral for the debt on Instagram and described her struggle:

DING DONG MY DEBTS ARE DEAD. . . . Let me tell you about my journey. . . . I wanted to start saving for my future. A house. Kids. A life. So I made a decision—I'd become debt-free by 30. I'm proud to say I accomplished my goal 2 years early. . . . I cut my budget and lived off of less than a third of my monthly salary. . . . I worked three jobs at once, my day job and then side hustles. I walked dogs until my feet literally bled. In the cold. In the rain. In the heat. Nothing was beneath me. I babysat. I cat sat. I stayed up for 24 hours straight to make a few hundred bucks as a TV extra on shows they filmed overnight. I cut my food budget down to merely salad, eggs, chicken and rice. . . . Was it easy? No. Worth it? I'm smiling in a cemetery. 102K lifted from my back. You tell me.

Quoted in Bre Avery, "This Woman Held a Funeral on Instagram After Paying Off Her 102K of Student Debt & She's Sharing How She Did It," Chip Chick, 2019. www.chipchick.com.

Freeing the Mind

Those who identify themselves as financially responsible do not make excuses or blame others when they need to fix past mistakes. They stick to the promise they make to themselves to stop wasting money. And they separate wants from needs and learn not to spend money when they are bored or lonely. Happily, there is a reward for developing positive financial habits: freedom. As money author Vicki Robin says, "Financial freedom is like freeing your mind. It is understanding that . . . there's an economy out there and I have a relationship with it, but it doesn't run my life."[44] As Robin sees it, taking control of spending is beneficial to both your bank account and your psychological well-being. And the world of banking and finance offers second chances to those willing to learn from their past mistakes and practice ways to ensure they are financially healthy in the future.

> "Financial freedom is like freeing your mind. It is understanding that . . . there's an economy out there and I have a relationship with it, but it doesn't run my life."[44]
>
> —Vicki Robin, money author

Source Notes

Introduction: Take Control or Be Controlled

1. Quoted in Opportunity Financial, "7 Expert Perspectives on Why Financial Literacy Is Important," 2020. www.opploans.com.

Chapter One: Where Do I Start?

2. Quoted in Eliza Brooke, "Juuls, Glossier, and Thrift Store Clothes: 6 High Schoolers on What They're Buying Right Now," Vox, September 24, 2018. www.vox.com.
3. Quoted in Brooke, "Juuls, Glossier, and Thrift Store Clothes."
4. LaToya Irby, "Tips for Teaching Your Child About Using a Credit Card," The Balance, September 9, 2019. www.thebalance.com.
5. Quoted in T. Rowe Price, "Parents Are Likely to Pass Down Good and Bad Financial Habits to Their Kids," March 23, 2017. www.troweprice.com.
6. Quoted in Melissa Lambarena, "How to Decipher the Fine Print on Your Credit Card Terms," MarketWatch, October 1, 2019. www.marketwatch.com.
7. Irby, "Tips for Teaching Your Child About Using a Credit Card."

Chapter Two: Building a Credit History

8. Quoted in Emma Sarran Webster, "Credit 101: Everything You Need to Know About Credit, Credit History, and Credit Scores," Teen Vogue, April 12, 2018. www.teenvogue.com.
9. Quoted in TechCrunch, "Step Raises $22.5M Led by Stripe to Build No-Fee Banking Services for Teens," June 6, 2019. https://techcrunch.com.

10. Justin Pritchard, "How to Get Debit Cards," The Balance, March 3, 2020. www.thebalance.com.

11. Quoted in Elizabeth Gravier, "The Secret to Going from a Credit Score in the Low 600s to Excellent—Without Ever Really Checking It," CNBC, April 27, 2020. www.cnbc.com.

12. Quoted in Gravier, "The Secret to Going from a Credit Score in the Low 600s to Excellent—Without Ever Really Checking It."

13. Quoted in Casey Bond, "How to Keep Your Child's Credit Safe," *U.S. News & World Report*, September 24, 2018. https://creditcards.usnews.com.

Chapter Three: What You Need to Know About Credit Cards

14. Quoted in Ann Carrns, "Give Your Teenager a Credit Card? Some Financial Experts Say Yes," *New York Times*, August 16, 2019. www.nytimes.com.

15. Quoted in Herb Weisbaum, "How Young Is Too Young for a Kid to Have a Credit Card?," NBC News, August 6, 2019. www.nbcnews.com.

16. Chuck Bentley, "Cash Is King and Other Bad Financial Advice," Beliefnet, 2020. www.beliefnet.com.

17. Craig Ford, "10 Things to Be Certain Teens Know About Credit Cards," Cash Money Life, March 13, 2019. https://cashmoneylife.com.

18. Quoted in Chris Kissell, "The Pros and Cons of Credit Cards," *U.S. News & World Report*, March 13, 2018. https://creditcards.usnews.com.

19. John S. Kiernan, "What Is a Secured Credit Card?," WalletHub, January 13, 2020. https://wallethub.com.

Chapter Four: Loans for Cars and College

20. Miranda Marquit, "A Millennial's Guide to Getting Your First Car Loan," Credit.com, February 13, 2018. www.credit.com.

21. Quoted in Marquit, "A Millennial's Guide to Getting Your First Car Loan."

22. Ian Redman, "My Student Loan Story," Credit Abuse Resistance Education, June 19, 2019. https://care4yourfuture.org.

23. Redman, "My Student Loan Story."

24. Redman, "My Student Loan Story."

25. Redman, "My Student Loan Story."

26. Quoted in Anna Helhoski, "Students Missed Out on $2.6 Billion in Free College Money," NerdWallet, October 16, 2018. www.nerdwallet.com.

27. Quoted in Teddy Nykiel, "How to Use A Net Price Calculator," NerdWallet, March 18, 2019, www.nerdwallet.com.

28. Quoted in Andrew Kreighbaum, "How Families Navigate the Growing Cost of College," *Insider Higher Ed*, September 4, 2019. www.insidehighered.com.

Chapter Five: Fixing Money Mistakes

29. Quoted in Megan DeMatteo, "How This Money Expert Paid Off More than $50,000 in Credit Card Debt She Incurred While Dealing with Unemployment, Divorce, and Cancer," CNBC, June 19, 2020. www.cnbc.com.

30. Quoted in DeMatteo, "How This Money Expert Paid Off More than $50,000 in Credit Card Debt She Incurred While Dealing with Unemployment, Divorce, and Cancer."

31. Quoted in DeMatteo, "How This Money Expert Paid Off More than $50,000 in Credit Card Debt She Incurred While Dealing with Unemployment, Divorce, and Cancer."

32. Quoted in A.J. Horch, "Almost Half of America Is Now Carrying Credit Card Debt, and More of It," CNBC, May 4, 2020. www.cnbc.com.

33. Quoted in Erica Sandberg, "How to Deal with Creditors When You Can't Pay," CreditCards.com, June 23, 2020. www.creditcards.com.

34. Quoted in Sandberg, "How to Deal with Creditors When You Can't Pay."

35. Quoted in Consolidated Credit, "Teenagers & Credit Cards," 2020. www.consolidatedcredit.org.

Chapter Six: Practice Makes Perfect

36. Quoted in ScienceDaily, "Parents: To Prepare Kids Financially, Give Them Practice with Money," November 27, 2018. www .sciencedaily.com.

37. Quoted in ScienceDaily, "Parents."

38. Liz Knueven, "How to Save Money as a Teenager So You Can Get Yourself a Car, Pay for College, or Take a Trip," Business Insider, March 5, 2020. www.businessinsider.com.

39. Quoted in Carrie Sloan, "4 Psychological Tricks That Can Banish Bad Money Habits," *Forbes*, July 29, 2013. www .forbes.com.

40. Quoted in Holly Quinn, "The Fintech App Serves Gen Z on Their Own Terms," Technical.ly, December 12, 2019. https:// technical.ly.

41. Quoted in Quinn, "The Fintech App Serves Gen Z on Their Own Terms."

42. Quoted in Quinn, "The Fintech App Serves Gen Z on Their Own Terms."

43. Quoted in NerdWallet, "Credit Card Fails: Confessions from NerdWallet's Experts," February 1, 2019. www.nerdwallet .com.

44. Quoted in Nicole Bayes-Fleming, "Spark Joy by Getting Rid of Bad Money Habits," Mindful, February 1, 2019. www.mindful .org.

For Further Research

Books

Corona Brezina and Barbara Gottfried, *What You Need to Know About Stocks*. New York: Rosen, 2020.

Josh Burnette and Pete Hardesty, *Adulting 101: #Wisdom 4Life*. Savage, MN: Broadstreet, 2018.

Tammy Gagne, *Credit Cards and Loans*. San Diego, CA: BrightPoint, 2020.

Erin Lowry, *Broke Millennial: Stop Scraping By and Get Your Financial Life Together*. New York: Random House, 2017.

Jason Porterfield, *What You Need to Know About Mortgages*. New York: Rosen, 2020.

Tim Wuebker, *Money for Teens: A Guide for Life*. Self-published, 2019.

Internet Sources

Anna Helhoski, "Students Missed Out on $2.6 Billion in Free College Money," NerdWallet, October 16, 2018. www.nerdwallet.com.

Latoya Irby, "Tips for Teaching Your Child About Using a Credit Card," The Balance, September 9, 2019. www.thebalance.com.

Andrew Kreighbaum, "How Families Navigate the Growing Cost of College," *Insider Higher Ed*, September 4, 2019. www.insidehighered.com.

Gabrielle Olya, "How to Come Back from 10 Credit Horror Stories," Yahoo Finance, November 7, 2019. https://finance.yahoo.com.

Opportunity Financial, "7 Expert Perspectives on Why Financial Literacy Is Important," 2020. www.opploans.com.

Joe Pinsker, "Why So Many Americans Don't Talk About Money," *The Atlantic*, March 2, 2020. www.theatlantic.com.

Websites

The Balance (www.thebalance.com). This site offers more than ten thousand pages of content with practical advice focused on banking, credit, budgeting, paying for college, and investing.

Credit Abuse Resistance Education (https://care4yourfuture. org). This nonprofit organization with chapters located throughout the country is dedicated to providing financial literacy education to students and young adults through presentations and online consultations with volunteers.

Money Under 30 (www.moneyunder30.com). This site offers personal financial information about banking, credit cards, loans, investing, and insurance to young adults who want to make good decisions about where their money goes.

NerdWallet (www.nerdwallet.com). This site offers comprehensive educational information about credit cards, banking, student loans, mortgages, and other financial matters, with a focus on those in the Gen Z and millennial demographic.

ScholarMe (www.scholarme.co). This company, founded by a high school student in 2018, is a free, one-stop-shop students can use to apply for college scholarships, student loans, and other sources of college funding.

Young Adult Money (www.youngadultmoney.com). Young Adult Money provides student-focused information about credit cards, student loans, saving money, and managing debt.

Index

Picture Credits

About the Author

Stuart A. Kallen is the author of more than 350 nonfiction books for children and young adults. He has written on topics ranging from the theory of relativity to the art of electronic dance music. In 2018 Kallen won a Green Earth Book Award from the Nature Generation environmental organization for his book *Trashing the Planet: Examining the Global Garbage Glut*. In his spare time he is a singer, songwriter, and guitarist in San Diego.